Robin Hood

Retold by Gina **D. B. Clemen**

Illustrated by Giovanni Manna

Editors: Michela Bruzzo, Nora Nagy
Design and art direction: Nadia Maestri
Computer graphics: Simona Corniola
Picture research: Alice Graziotin

© 2012 Black Cat
First edition: January 2012

Picture credits: Photos.com; IstockPhoto; DreamsTime; Charles Marie Rigobert Bonne/Getty Images: 6; Bridgeman Art Library/Getty images: 8; Bettmann/CORBIS: 9; Heritage Images/Corbis: 10; Tips Images: 31; Tips Images: 62; Stapleton Collection/Corbis: 63; Bettmann/CORBIS: 77; Heritage Images/Corbis: 87; Webphoto: 90-91.

All rights reserved. No part of this book may be reproduced, stored in a retrieval system, or transmitted, in any form or by any means, electronic, mechanical, photocopying, recording or otherwise, without the written permission of the publisher.

We would be happy to receive your comments and suggestions, and give you any other information concerning our material.
info@blackcat-cideb.com
blackcat-cideb.com

The Publisher is certified by

 CISQCERT

in compliance with the UNI EN ISO 9001:2008 standards for the activities of «Design and production of educational materials» (certificate no. 02.565)

ISBN 978-88-530-1207-4   Book + audio CD/CD-ROM

Printed in Italy by Italgrafica, Novara

The CD contains an audio section (the recording of the text) and a CD-ROM section (additional games and activities that practise the four skills).
- To listen to the recording, insert the CD into your CD player and it will play as normal. You can also listen to the recording on your computer, by opening your usual CD player program.
- If you put the CD directly into the CD-ROM drive, the software will open automatically.

SYSTEM REQUIREMENTS for CD-ROM	
PC: • Pentium III processor • Windows 98, 2000 or XP • 64 Mb RAM (128Mb RAM recommended) • 800x600 screen resolution 16 bit • 12X CD-ROM drive • Audio card with speakers or headphones	**Macintosh:** • Power PC G3 or above (G4 recommended) • Mac OS 10.1.5 • 128 Mb RAM free for the application
All the trademarks above are copyright.	

Contents

Introduction		5
Robin Hood Country		6
CHAPTER ONE	How Robin Became an Outlaw	13
CHAPTER TWO	Friar Tuck	21
CHAPTER THREE	Maid Marian	36
CHAPTER FOUR	The Cowardly Sheriff	44
CHAPTER FIVE	The Archery Contest	53
CHAPTER SIX	Alice and Alan	67
CHAPTER SEVEN	A Knight in the Forest	80
DOSSIERS	Medieval Times in England	8
	Medieval Life in a Castle Town	29
	Archery	62
	King Richard's Crusade	76
	The Magna Carta	87
	Filmography	90

UNDERSTANDING THE TEXT   18, 26, 41, 49, 59, 72, 84

PET PET-style activities   18, 26, 27, 35, 42, 43, 49, 50, 52, 66, 72, 79, 84, 85, 92

T: GRADE 4   Trinity-style activities (Grade 4)   41, 61

PROJECTS ON THE WEB   11, 20, 34, 51, 65, 89

AFTER READING   92

The text is recorded in full.
 These symbols indicate the beginning and end of the passages linked to the listening activities.

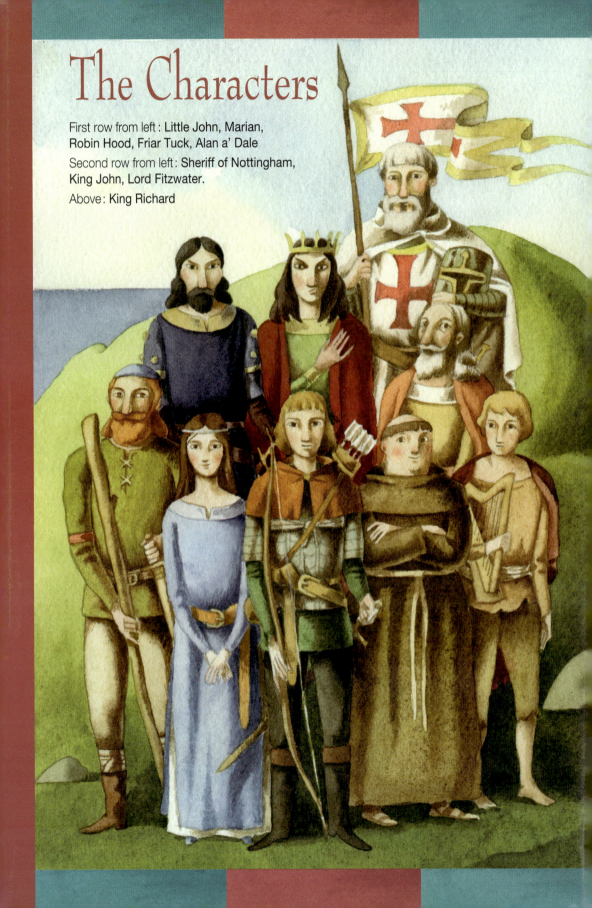

The Characters

First row from left: **Little John, Marian, Robin Hood, Friar Tuck, Alan a' Dale**

Second row from left: **Sheriff of Nottingham, King John, Lord Fitzwater.**

Above: **King Richard**

Introduction

What is a legend?

A legend is a very old and popular story that may be true. A legend sometimes begins as a true story, but as the years pass some things are added to it and other things are forgotten. So, a legend is a mix of historical facts and popular fantasy.

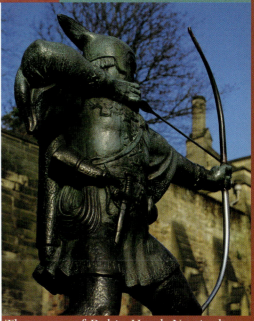

The statue of Robin Hood, Nottingham.

Who was Robin Hood?

Everyone has heard of the outlaw [1] Robin Hood who lived in Sherwood Forest. No other outlaw in history or literature is as famous as Robin Hood. People everywhere love this colourful hero and his men.

No one knows for certain who Robin Hood was. Legend tells us that Robin Hood lived in the late 12th century at the time of King Richard the Lionheart in Sherwood Forest near the town of Nottingham.

In the records of the English courts of 1225 there was a real outlaw named Robert Hood. In the 15th century ballads [2] about Robin's life and adventures became well known and the earliest text of a Robin Hood ballad was 'Robin Hood and the Monk'. This ancient manuscript was written shortly after 1450 and is now kept in Cambridge University, England.

During the Victorian Age, Howard Pyle wrote *The Merry Adventures of Robin Hood* (1883) which became very popular and influenced most of the versions of the legend of Robin Hood throughout the 20th century.

1. **outlaw** : a person who lives outside the protection of the law; a criminal.
2. **ballads** : songs that tell stories.

Robin Hood Country

The adventures of Robin Hood and his outlaws took place in central England, in Sherwood Forest and Nottingham. These are real places, although the forest has become much smaller and Nottingham has become much bigger since Robin's time.

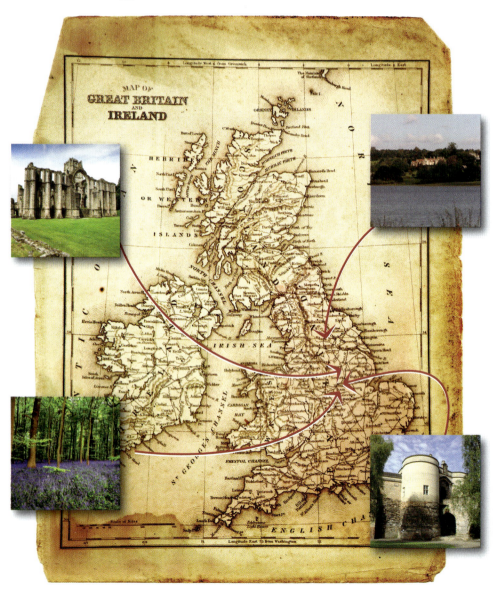

1 LISTENING

  You're going to take a tour of Robin Hood Country with a tour guide. You will hear the guide telling you about tour times, meals and some special places. For each question fill in the missing information in the numbered space.

Robin Hood Country Tour

Tour guide
Her name is (1) ....
Her office is (2) ....

Tour times
Bus tour starts at (3) ....
Ticket prices: (4) ....for adults and
(5)........................ for children.

Meals
Packed lunches:
Regular meal: (6) ...., cheeseburger, fries, soda, (7) .... , chocolate biscuits
Kids' meal: hamburger, (8) ....,
(9) .... , biscuits

Tour
Fountains Abbey
Founded in (10) ....by
(11) .... monks.

Barnsdale Forest
One of Robin Hood's outlaws,
(12) .... , came from Barnsdale.

View of a city with labourers paving roads while the king stands in a chamber dictating to two scribes (15th century).

Medieval Times in England

After the Battle of Hastings in 1066, the Normans conquered and controlled England. The Normans were people from Normandy, a region in north-west France and their leader, William, Duke of Normandy, became William I, King of England.

The story of Robin Hood is set in medieval times when England was under Norman rule. In these times there was the feudal system in Western Europe which meant that all the land in the country belonged to the king. However, since the king could not live on all his land he let noblemen use it. These were people from high society and knights. The king also gave land to important religious leaders.

In return these people protected the king and gave him money. When there was a battle or a war the knights went to fight for their king. Kings and noblemen lived in big castles from which they could control the peasants.

People who were not noble were called peasants and they paid money to the nobleman to live on his land. They also grew food and had to give most of it to the nobleman. These peasants were very poor, had no rights and led a difficult life. These were times of great social injustice, as you will see in the story you are going to read.

Peasants farming outside the castle (circa late 15th century).

Knights jousting at a tournament in the 12th century (circa 1815).

In medieval times, England was divided into counties, or shires, such as Nottinghamshire. Each county had a sheriff who was chosen by the king. He had to collect taxes and carry out the decisions of the king. A sheriff had a number of men to help him do his work. When the king was away the sheriff and his men sometimes became cruel and dishonest.

1 COMPREHENSION CHECK
Answer these questions.

1. Who were the Normans and when did they conquer England?
2. What was the feudal system?
3. What did the peasants do with most of the food they grew?
4. Who chose the sheriff of a county?
5. What was the sheriff's job?

PROJECT ON THE WEB

Feudalism in England

Connect to the Internet and search for information about feudalism in England.

Work in small groups and answer these questions:

1. When was feudalism introduced in England?
2. Who was William the Conqueror?
3. What was the Domesday Book?
4. Did the Anglo-Saxons fight against the Normans?
5. What did feudalism mean to the English peasants?
6. How did the Normans maintain feudalism in England?

BEFORE YOU READ

1 VOCABULARY

Match the words with their meaning. Use a dictionary only if necessary.

1. ☐ greedy
2. ☐ slaves
3. ☐ earl
4. ☐ merchants
5. ☐ staff
6. ☐ stream
7. ☐ cave

A the title of a nobleman
B a very small river
C people who sell things to others
D people who are not free
E a big wooden stick
F a large hole in the side of a hill
G when you want to have more and more, and you never share anything

2 WORD SQUARE

Now circle the seven new words from exercise 1 in the word square.

A	Q	E	R	S	Y	U	I	O	P	J
M	N	M	V	C	L	S	A	Q	W	G
M	Z	L	E	J	H	A	F	D	S	R
C	E	B	N	R	L	K	V	P	U	E
M	A	B	C	C	Z	A	E	W	E	
U	R	N	A	H	B	H	K	M	S	D
Q	L	W	V	T	Y	U	A	O	P	Y
C	V	B	E	B	G	F	D	N	Y	U
L	L	P	O	I	F	K	M	N	T	H
P	L	M	O	F	N	B	J	I	J	S
A	D	F	A	H	B	N	M	L	P	O
M	N	T	G	B	S	T	R	E	A	M
M	S	S	Z	X	C	W	E	D	F	R
W	E	S	O	I	J	K	L	P	M	N

3 READING PICTURES

Look at the picture on page 15 and answer the following questions.

1. Where are the men sitting?
2. What is the man on the tree doing?
3. What do you think Robin Hood is saying?

CHAPTER **ONE**

How Robin Became an Outlaw

At the time of this story King Richard, known as the Lionheart because of his bravery, was away on a crusade in the Holy Land. During this time his brother, the greedy Prince John, ruled England in his place and no one liked him. Although John was a prince and not a king, people called him King John when he was ruling England. Prince John made the people pay very high taxes and took away their lands and belongings. Poor peasants often died of hunger. The sheriff of Nottingham was one of Prince John's worst sheriffs. These were very difficult times.

Robin Hood's real name was Robert, son of the Earl of Huntingdon, a tall, handsome young man. He was kind and friendly with everyone. One day the cruel sheriff of Nottingham killed Robin's father in order to take away his many lands in Locksley.

Robin Hood

Young Robin lost his father, his home, his belongings and all his lands. He was very upset because he loved his father very much.

'What can I do?' he thought. 'I'm alone and I don't have my family or my home any more.'

Robin decided to escape to Sherwood Forest with his faithful servants. They chose to live as free men in the forest, although they lived outside the law. They did not want to be slaves of King John and the evil sheriff of Nottingham. However, King John considered them dangerous outlaws and enemies of England.

Deep inside the forest Robin sat under a huge old oak tree [1] and talked to his faithful servants.

'Sherwood Forest is our new home. We'll live in the caves that are warm and dry in the winter and cool in the summer. We'll hunt the animals of the forest and go fishing in the streams. We'll wear green clothes, the same colour as the trees, and carry bows and arrows. [2] When I blow my horn [3] three times, you must all hurry to my side.'

'It sounds good!' said his men, who sat listening to him.

'But remember, my friends, we are free but we are outlaws,' said Robin seriously. 'We are considered dangerous enemies of England – the rich and the greedy hate us and are against us. Only the poor honest people are with us.'

'We understand,' they all said.

'I'll always stay with you but you must do what I tell you. Remember, we are good, honest men. We must never hurt the poor, the old or women and children. We must help and protect them. Do you agree?'

1. **oak tree :**
2. **bows and arrows :**
3. **horn :**

Robin Hood

'Yes, we do!' cried his men.

'This is my plan,' said Robin. 'We'll only take from rich noblemen, dishonest merchants and greedy churchmen. When rich travellers come through Sherwood Forest we'll invite them to eat with us, but they must pay for their meal. We'll then give this money to the poor. Do you all promise to do what I tell you?'

'Yes, we do,' shouted his men happily.

Soon the rich and greedy noblemen and merchants were afraid to travel through Sherwood Forest alone. They always travelled with a small army of men for protection because they knew that the price for Robin's meal was high. Some people called this the Sherwood Tax.

Other brave and honest men heard about Robin and his men and they soon joined the outlaws: Much, Nat, Will Scarlet and others. All the men were excellent archers but Robin Hood was the best archer of all. They often practised in the forest with their bows and arrows.

The peasants in the nearby villages and in Nottingham knew about the outlaws of Sherwood Forest and liked them. They often hid them from the sheriff's men and offered them bread and soup. In return the outlaws often gave the peasants fish from the streams.

One day while Robin was walking in Sherwood Forest he came to a stream with a narrow wooden bridge. He began to cross it when he saw a huge man on the other side of the stream.

'This man is a giant,' Robin thought. 'He's very tall and strong and he's carrying a wooden staff.'

'Step back and let me cross the bridge first,' shouted the stranger who was a bit older than Robin.

'No, I was here first,' shouted Robin, looking at the stranger.

'Well, if you're strong enough to knock me off the bridge then you can cross first,' said the huge man with a loud voice. 'You have a sword but I only have a staff.'

How Robin Became an Outlaw

Robin took his sword and cut a long branch from a tree and made a long staff.

'Very well,' said Robin, 'I'm ready to fight. Let's see who's the strongest! The winner will be the one who knocks the other into the water.'

'Alright, I agree,' said the tall stranger.

The two men got onto the narrow bridge and walked towards each other slowly. When they reached the middle they started fighting. Robin was light and moved quickly but the other man was much stronger. Suddenly the stranger pushed Robin off the bridge and into the cold water of the stream. The stranger started laughing and pulled Robin out of the water.

'You beat me!' said Robin laughing. 'You're a strong fighter. What's your name?'

'My name's John Little and I'm from Barnsdale,' said the stranger smiling. 'I'm looking for Robin Hood because I want to join his outlaws who live somewhere in this forest. I'm an honest man and a good archer. I don't want to live under King John's rule; he's a cruel, greedy man. And his sheriff is even worse!'

'Welcome to Sherwood Forest! I'm Robin Hood!' said Robin happily. 'We need strong men and good archers.'

The two men laughed and became good friends.

'Now you're one of our outlaws and you must change your name,' said Robin, thinking of another name. 'Your new name will be… Little John.'

Robin introduced Little John to the other outlaws who were glad to welcome the new outlaw. That evening they enjoyed a big meal around the fire, telling stories and laughing.

UNDERSTANDING THE TEXT

1 COMPREHENSION CHECK
Choose the correct answer – A, B, C or D.

1 Prince John ruled England
   A ☐ and everyone liked and admired him.
   B ☐ and people called him Lionheart because of his bravery.
   C ☐ because his brother was away from England.
   D ☐ for only three months.

2 Robin Hood grew up in
   A ☐ Locksley.
   B ☐ Barnsdale.
   C ☐ Nottingham.
   D ☐ Sherwood Forest.

3 The Sherwood Tax
   A ☐ was the Sheriff of Nottingham's highest tax.
   B ☐ was the price of a meal with Robin and his outlaws.
   C ☐ was paid by all the peasants in Nottingham.
   D ☐ was paid to King Richard before going on a crusade.

4 Robin Hood and Little John
   A ☐ fought on the bridge with their swords.
   B ☐ fought in the forest with bows and arrows.
   C ☐ fought on the bridge with their staffs.
   D ☐ didn't fight because they were good friends.

5 John Little was from
   A ☐ Barnsdale.
   B ☐ Nottingham.
   C ☐ Sherwood Forest.
   D ☐ Locksley.

6 The outlaws promised Robin Hood
   A ☐ to go hunting in the forest every day.
   B ☐ to meet under the old oak tree twice a week.
   C ☐ to build new homes in Sherwood Forest.
   D ☐ to take from the rich and give to the poor.

2 VOCABULARY

A Circle the word that doesn't belong and explain why.

1. greedy   cruel   dishonest   kind
2. Earl   brother   King   Prince
3. protect   attack   help   defend
4. meal   breakfast   dinner   lunch
5. England   France   English   Turkey
6. upset   worried   unhappy   tired
7. fast   quickly   slowly   immediately

B Use the odd words to complete the sentences.

1. The outlaws enjoyed a good .... by the fire.
2. Robin Hood was a .... man.
3. The .... people didn't like King John.
4. John was King Richard's ....
5. The old man walked .... because his legs hurt.
6. The peasants were .... after a long day at work.
7. The sheriff's men started to .... the poor peasants.

3 QUESTION WORDS

Complete the questions with *why, how, what, who* or *where* and then choose the correct answer below.

1. .... did Robin Hood and the outlaws live?
2. .... was King Richard's brother?
3. .... did Little John leave Barnsdale?
4. .... did rich noblemen and dishonest merchants travel through Sherwood Forest?
5. .... was Little John's staff made of?

A ☐ He left because he didn't want to live under King John's rule.
B ☐ They travelled through Sherwood Forest with a small army of men for protection.
C ☐ They lived in Sherwood Forest.
D ☐ Wood.
E ☐ Prince John.

PROJECT ON THE WEB

The Major Oak and Sherwood Forest today

Connect to the Internet and search for information about the Major Oak and Sherwood Forest.

The Major Oak is the legendary oak tree where *Robin Hood* and his outlaws used to meet and talk. Today this beautiful old tree is a famous tourist attraction. Work in small groups and answer these questions:

1 Where is the Major Oak located?
2 What are its dimensions?
3 What does the Domesday Book say about Sherwood Forest?
4 What are the theories about this extraordinary tree?
5 How is Sherwood Forest taking care of the Major Oak?

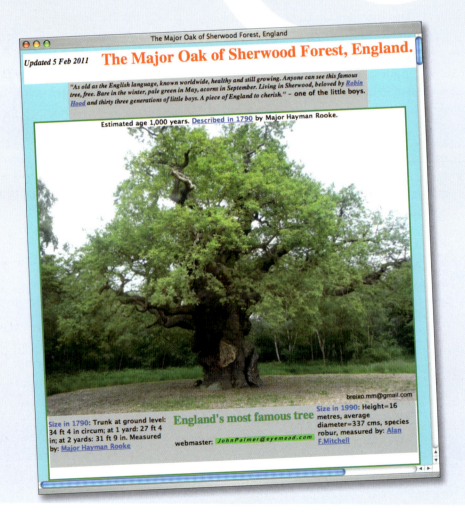

CHAPTER **TWO**

Friar[1] Tuck

'Robin, did you know that a big man who looks like a friar lives alone in a little cave by the stream in our forest?' asked Will Scarlett.

'Are you sure he's a friar?' asked Robin, surprised.

'Well, he wears sandals and brown clothes like a friar,' said Will Scarlett.

'Tomorrow I'll go and see this man,' said Robin.

Early the next morning Robin started looking for the friar. He walked along the stream and soon found the friar, who was a big, tall man of about fifty.

'Good morning,' said Robin.

'Good morning, young man,' said the friar.

'Do you know that you're fishing in an outlaw stream?' asked Robin.

1. friar :

Robin Hood

'What! An outlaw stream? What do you mean?' asked the friar who was quite confused.

'Yes, this stream belongs to the outlaws of Sherwood Forest, and the fish you catch are ours. However, you can fish here once a month if you carry me across the stream on your back.'

'I certainly don't like the way this young man talks to me,' thought the angry friar. 'The stream belongs to everyone.'

'Well,' said the friar, 'I can certainly carry you across the stream because you're thin. But can you carry me across the stream? Are you strong enough?'

'Of course I'm strong enough,' said Robin. 'I'm thin but I'm very strong.' Robin lifted the heavy man with great difficulty but he was able to carry him across the stream.

'Alright, friar, I carried you and now you must carry me,' said Robin, who was tired.

The friar easily lifted Robin and started carrying him across the stream, but when they got to the middle the friar suddenly stopped. The friar smelled Robin and cried, 'Goodness! You smell like an old rat! You really need a bath!' He started laughing and threw Robin into the cold water of the stream.

The friar continued laughing and pulled Robin out of the stream. Robin was very cold and angry at first, but then he looked at the friar's kind eyes and said, 'You were right, I needed a bath! And you can fish in the stream whenever you want.'

'What's your name, young man?' asked the friar, who was smiling at Robin.

'My name's Robin Hood,' said Robin.

'You're Robin Hood!' exclaimed the friar, surprised. 'Let's shake hands and be friends. I'm Michael Tuck, a friar from Fountains Abbey.'

Robin Hood

'Why are you living in a cave in the forest?' asked Robin.

'I had a big quarrel [2] with the head of Fountains Abbey,' said the friar. 'He was greedy and wanted to be rich. He never helped the poor peasants. I didn't like him so I escaped from the abbey and now I lead a simple, honest life.'

'Why don't you come and join me and my outlaws in the middle of the forest?' said Robin, smiling at his new friend. 'We are all good men and you'll be happy with us, Friar Tuck!'

Robin took Friar Tuck's huge hand and shook it. They were now friends forever.

The months passed and many other honest men joined the outlaws of Sherwood Forest. There were probably more than 200 in all and they lived together happily. Robin became the hero of the poor, the peasants, the women and children. He took from the rich and the greedy and gave to the poor.

King John and the evil [3] sheriff of Nottingham were very angry with Robin and the outlaws.

'It has become very dangerous for noblemen, merchants and churchmen to travel across Sherwood Forest,' said King John angrily. 'Sheriff, you must do something to stop Robin Hood and his outlaws!'

'I'll send a big army of my best soldiers to Sherwood Forest,' said the sheriff of Nottingham, 'and they'll find those outlaws and arrest them!'

The sheriff's army went to Sherwood Forest and looked everywhere for the outlaws, but they didn't look up in the tall trees. Robin and the outlaws were hiding there, and jumped down and fought against the soldiers, killing all except one. Robin and his men were the brave fighters.

'Listen to me,' said Robin to the only soldier who was still

---

2. **quarrel** : argument, disagreement.   3. **evil** : very bad.

Friar Tuck

alive, 'go back to the sheriff and tell him that we're not afraid of anyone and he can't stop us! Do you understand?'

'Ah...yes, sir, I understand,' said the soldier who was terribly frightened. He got on his horse and galloped away into the forest.

No one could stop Robin and his men. King John and the sheriff were furious because the people laughed at them. King John was also furious because his people hated him and loved his brother, King Richard the Lionheart.

'I have to stop Robin Hood,' shouted King John to the sheriff. 'He's my worst nightmare![4] Don't you have any ideas? Use your head!'

The sheriff thought for a minute or two and said, 'Why don't we offer a reward? The reward will be one hundred pieces of gold for Robin Hood, dead or alive!'

'That's a great idea!' cried King John. 'Why didn't I think of it? Tomorrow I'll make an announcement to the people of Nottingham.'

The next day the king stood on the tall castle walls and spoke to a big crowd of people. 'Robin Hood and his outlaws are our dangerous enemies. I'll pay one hundred pieces of gold for Robin, dead or alive!'

The people in the crowd were surprised and started talking.

'One hundred pieces of gold!' exclaimed a young merchant to his wife. 'That's a lot of money. We can buy many beautiful things with all that gold.'

'You're right,' said his young wife, 'we can buy new clothes, new furniture, another horse and jewels for me...'

'All we have to do is find Robin Hood!' said the greedy young merchant.

The poor peasants listened to the king and were very sad, because Robin Hood was their hero and they wanted to help and protect him.

---

4. **nightmare** : a very bad, scary dream.

UNDERSTANDING THE TEXT

1 COMPREHENSION CHECK

Read the sentences below and decide if each sentence is correct or incorrect. If it is correct, mark A. If it is not correct, mark B.

                                      A B

1. Will Scarlett told Robin Hood about a man who wanted to cross the bridge over the stream.
2. The big, tall man near the stream was a friar of about fifty.
3. Robin Hood told the friar that he could fish in the stream once a week.
4. Robin Hood carried the friar across the stream very easily.
5. The friar threw Robin Hood into the cold stream because he smelled bad.
6. Robin Hood got angry and started fighting with the friar.
7. The friar's name was Michael Tuck and he didn't like the head of Fountains Abbey.
8. The Sheriff of Nottingham's army could not find Robin Hood and the outlaws in Sherwood Forest.
9. The Sheriff of Nottingham decided to offer a reward of ten pieces of gold for Robin Hood, dead or alive.
10. The peasants of Nottingham wanted to find Robin Hood because they needed the ten pieces of gold.

2 SENTENCE TRANSFORMATION

For each question, complete the second so that it means the same as the first, using no more than three words. There's an example at the beginning.

0. The town is called Nottingham.
   The ....*name of*............... the town is Nottingham.

1. King John was very unpopular.
   No one .... King John.

2. King Richard's crusade lasted four years.
   King Richard was .... years.

3. It wasn't easy to travel through Sherwood Forest.
   It was .... through Sherwood Forest.

4. There were only a few outlaws in the forest.
   There weren't .... outlaws in the forest.

5. Little John was the only person in the cave.
   There was .... in the cave except Little John.

3 SOME AND ANY

Look at the rules for using *some* and *any*. Then complete the sentences below.

> **SOME**
> (something, someone, somebody, somewhere)
> generally used in affirmative phrases
>
> *He found some apples on the tree.*
> *They were talking to someone in town.*
>
> **ANY**
> (anything, anyone, anybody, anywhere)
> generally used in questions and negative phrases with *not*
>
> *Is there any water on the table?*
> *We didn't see anyone in the forest.*

1 Robin Hood went to the forest with .... of his faithful servants.
2 The poor peasants didn't have .... to eat.
3 Does she have .... money?
4 The outlaws were hiding .... in the forest.
5 They didn't drink .... because they weren't thirsty.
6 Little John had .... in his hand.

4 WRITING

Friar Tuck wants to write a card to his good friend, Friar Matthew, at Fountains Abbey.

In the card Friar Tuck wants to tell him:
- why he decided to leave Fountains Abbey
- how he met Robin Hood
- about his life in Sherwood Forest

Start like this:

> Dear Friar Matthew,
> Last month I decided to leave Fountains Abbey because…

Use about 35-45 words.

5 CHARACTERS

Write a brief description of each character using some of the words in the box below. You can use the same words more than once.

cruel   kind   strong   tall   big   dishonest   greedy   thin
friendly   brave   honest   evil   handsome   young

Robin Hood

....
....
....
....

Little John

....
....
....
....

Friar Tuck

....
....
....
....

King John

....
....
....
....

Sheriff of Nottingham

....
....
....
....

Bodiam Castle

Medieval Life in a Castle Town

Before the Norman invasion the castles in England were small wooden buildings which were not strong and were at a high risk of fire. They were usually built on small hills.

The Normans instead built big stone castles with thick walls because they were strong, difficult to attack and did not burn. One of the first Norman stone castles was the Tower of London which was started in 1078.

Castles and towns

In the Middle Ages people often built their houses near a castle and this is how towns developed. The castle, which usually belonged to a lord or a king, offered protection during attacks by enemies since it was defended by soldiers. When there was any kind of danger, the people of the town ran to the castle because they were safe inside its walls and there was plenty of food and drink for many days.

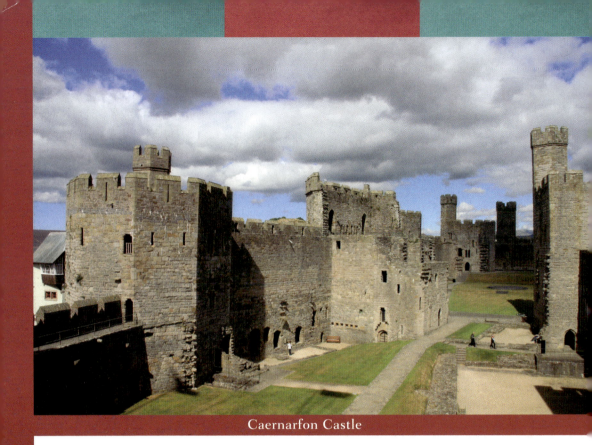
Caernarfon Castle

Sometimes the castle was built long after the town had developed and the castle walls surrounded and protected the town. The people of the town paid rent to the lord of the castle and were loyal to him.

Towns were often built near rivers which offered drinking water and a means of transportation. Castles were usually built in places that were difficult to attack: near the sea or on high hills or mountains. In this way the soldiers could easily see the enemy arriving.

In the Middle Ages town streets were very muddy and dirty since there was no sewer system.[1] And they were very smelly too, because rubbish was thrown out of the windows and was left in the streets. Luckily, pigs, dogs and birds ate some of the rubbish and helped clean the town, but there were always lots of rats.[2]

1. **sewer system** : an underground system that carries rain water and waste away.
2. **rats** :

Market day in town

Most castle towns held a big market once or twice a week. On market day the town square was filled with crowds of people and merchants who were selling their goods. Visitors to the market could buy almost anything: shoes, cloth, candles, bowls, knives and swords.

A few times a year there was also a fair, which was much bigger than the weekly market and sold many more goods from far away places. The word 'fair' comes from the Latin word 'feria', which meant a holiday, when people didn't work. Of course, this was the best time to have a fair because most people were free to attend.

Fairs usually lasted several days and attracted merchants from other countries who sold carpets from Turkey, fine cloth and beautiful glassware from Italy, olive oil from Spain and Greece and other unusual things. It was often difficult to keep order at the fair

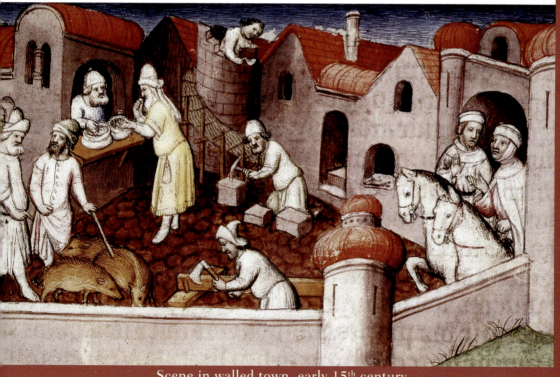

Scene in walled town, early 15th century.

because there were big crowds of people. Visitors to the fair had to be very careful because pickpockets, also known as 'cutpurses', cut off the purses that hung from people's belts.

Musicians, actors and acrobats

The days of the fair were always important ones and there were jugglers,[3] musicians, actors, acrobats and other entertainers. They often performed in the courtyards of inns. Since they could not sell tickets to their performance, they sent a hat around to collect money. In medieval times acting and entertaining were not considered serious jobs.

Town shops and guilds corporazioni (Trade Unions)

Craftsmen[4] had their shops around the town square. Since few people could read or write in the Middle Ages, special signs were hung outside the shops to show what was sold inside. For example, a pair of scissors was the sign for a shop that made and sold knives and scissors, and a green bush was the sign for an inn. al berghetto

In many towns craftsmen and merchants belonged to groups called guilds, which became powerful during the Middle Ages. There were several different kinds of guilds and each one had a special sign with symbols of its work. For example, the wheel-makers guild had a sign with a picture of four wheels.

The guilds controlled prices and protected the quality and secrets of their work. They also organised apprenticeships for young boys who wanted to learn a specific job. An apprentice was a young boy of about eleven or twelve who went to live with the family of a craftsman and learned the job. After seven years the apprentice was free to leave the craftsman and set up his own shop.

3. **jugglers** : giocoliere

4. **craftsmen** : people who make things with their hands and sell them.

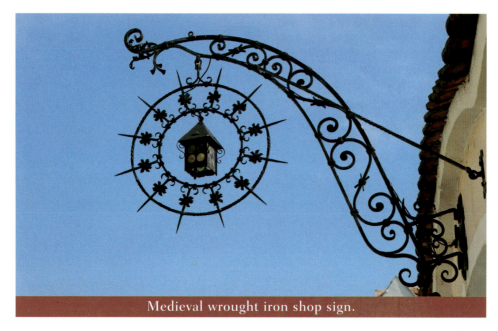

Medieval wrought iron shop sign.

Craftsmen's shops were usually found in one area of town. Some town streets still have the name of the craftsmen who worked there, such as Bread Street, which had bakeries, or Milk Street where the cows were kept.

1 COMPREHENSION CHECK
Are these statements true (T) or false (F)? Correct the false ones.

T F

1 After the Norman invasion most castles were made of wood. ☐ ☐
2 The lord of the castle asked the people of the town to pay rent. ☐ ☐
3 Castles that were built near the sea or in the mountains were difficult to defend. ☐ ☐
4 The towns of the Middle Ages were not clean places. ☐ ☐
5 The weekly market was smaller and less important than the fair. ☐ ☐
6 Shops had a sign outside with the name of the goods that were sold inside. ☐ ☐
7 Guilds were powerful organizations in the Middle Ages. ☐ ☐
8 An apprentice worked for eleven years with a craftsman before he could open a shop. ☐ ☐

PROJECT ON THE WEB

Let's learn more about guilds!

Connect to the Internet and search for information about medieval guilds.

Guilds were an important part of medieval society and became very powerful in local governments.

Work in small groups and answer one of the following questions:

1. What was a guild?
2. What was the purpose of a guild?
3. How did the guilds protect the workers and the guild members?
4. How did the guilds protect the consumers?
5. What was the difference between merchant guilds and craft guilds?

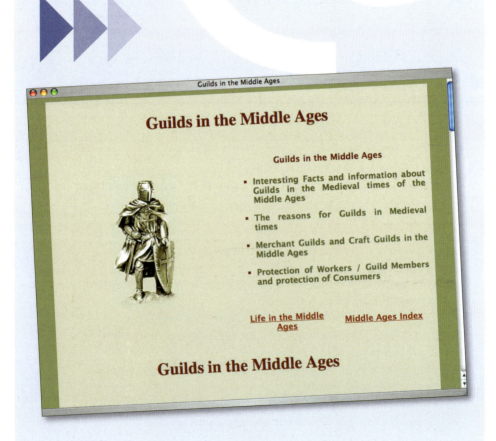

BEFORE YOU READ

1 LISTENING

Listen to the beginning of Chapter Three and choose the correct answer – A, B or C.

1. Marian and Mark Fitzwater were
   - A ☐ Robin's cousins.
   - B ☐ Robin's best friends.
   - C ☐ new outlaws.

2. Sir Guy of Gisbourne was
   - A ☐ Marian's brother.
   - B ☐ Mark's best friend.
   - C ☐ a rich nobleman.

3. Marian's father said that she
   - A ☐ must marry Sir Guy of Gisbourne.
   - B ☐ must marry the Sheriff of Nottingham.
   - C ☐ must learn to fight with a sword.

4. Mark decided to
   - A ☐ talk to Sir Guy of Gisbourne.
   - B ☐ disguise himself as a knight.
   - C ☐ disguise his sister as a knight.

5. Marian got to Sherwood Forest
   - A ☐ when it was almost dark.
   - B ☐ at night.
   - C ☐ early in the morning.

6. Robin Hood was disguised as a
   - A ☐ knight.
   - B ☐ beggar.
   - C ☐ friar.

2 READING PICTURES

Look at the picture on page 39 and answer the following questions.

1. Describe the scene. What time of the day is it? Where are Robin and Marian?
2. Describe Robin and Marian. What are they wearing? What are they doing?
3. Describe the expressions on Robin and Marian's faces.

CHAPTER **THREE**
Maid Marian

Robin Hood met Marian Fitzwater and her brother, Mark, when he was a boy. They were best friends and always played together. Robin taught Marian and Mark to use the bow and arrow and to fight with the sword. Marian loved Robin and he loved her.

A few years after Robin Hood became an outlaw, Marian's father wanted to talk to her about something important.

'Marian, you are young and beautiful,' said Lord Robert Fitzwater of Malaset. 'And you're very lucky because there is a rich and important nobleman who wants to marry you.'

Marian was worried and asked, 'Who is this rich nobleman?'

'His name is Sir Guy of Gisbourne, a rich nobleman from Gisborne. He's a good friend of the sheriff of Nottingham,' said Lord Robert, smiling at his daughter.

Maid Marian

'What! Sir Guy of Gisbourne!' cried Marian. 'He's almost twice my age and I don't love him!'

'Marian, listen to your father,' said Lord Robert. 'Sir Guy of Gisbourne is very important and rich. He'll be a fine husband for you and you'll live in his beautiful home in Gisbourne.'

'I don't want to marry him!' cried Marian loudly. 'I don't love him!'

'You will obey your father!' cried Lord Robert, whose face was red with anger. 'I know what's best for you. Now go back to your room and stay there!'

Marian's eyes were filled with tears as she ran back to her room. She sat on her bed and started crying. She didn't know what to do. Later that day she talked to her brother Mark and told him about the terrible situation.

'I'll never marry Sir Guy of Gisbourne,' said Marian. 'I've decided to run away and join Robin Hood in Sherwood Forest. He's the man I love and want to marry.'

Mark was very surprised but he understood his sister's feelings. 'I know you'll be happy with Robin. You've always loved him,' said Mark. 'I've got a clever idea – I can help you disguise [1] yourself as a knight with a sword. No one will recognise you and you can travel safely through the forest.'

'Oh, Mark, thank you!' said Marian smiling.

With her brother's help Marian disguised herself as a knight, got on her horse and left for Sherwood Forest. When she got to the big forest it was almost dark.

On the same day Robin Hood was in the forest, too. He was

---

1. **disguise** : change your appearance.

Robin Hood

coming from Nottingham disguised as a beggar.² As he was walking through the forest he saw a young knight approaching on a horse.

'What are you doing in the forest at this time?' asked Robin, looking at the young knight.

'What are you doing here, beggar man?' answered the knight.

Marian and Robin did not recognise each other.

'This is outlaw country and we don't like strangers on our land,' said Robin. 'Go back now before there's trouble.'

'I will not go back, beggar man!' said Marian angrily. 'I'm not afraid of anyone – certainly not of outlaws! I can fight you and win!'

'Really?' said Robin, surprised.

It was getting darker and darker in the forest when the fight began. Robin was an expert with the sword but Marian was very skilled, too. The fight went on for some time and suddenly Robin's foot hit a big stone and he fell to the ground.

Marian pointed her sword at his throat and said, 'You lost the fight. Take me to your leader, Robin Hood.' She took off her helmet³ and her long hair fell over her shoulders. Robin was amazed.

'You're Marian and I'm Robin Hood!' he exclaimed.

Marian was surprised and couldn't speak for a moment. 'It's you, Robin!' she cried happily. 'I didn't recognise you because you were disguised.'

'I have to disguise myself when I go to the village because King John and the sheriff want me, dead or alive!' said Robin, taking

2. **beggar** : a very poor person.   3. **helmet** :

Robin Hood

Marian's hand. They looked at each other and kissed. Robin and Marian were finally together.

'My father wanted me to marry Sir Guy of Gisbourne,' said Marian. 'I was very upset and I started crying, because I love only you, Robin.'

'And I love only you, dear Marian,' said Robin softly.

"I decided to disguise myself and look for you in Sherwood Forest,' said Marian. 'My brother Mark helped me.'

'I'm very happy because you're here with me, Marian,' said Robin. 'Come, let's go and meet the outlaws. I know you'll like them and they'll like you!'

Robin took Marian to meet his men in the forest. Everyone was delighted to meet Marian who was friendly and kind, and there was a very special dinner that evening. After dinner everyone sat around the fire and sang happy songs.

'When is the wedding day?' asked Friar Tuck, smiling.

'The day after tomorrow!' said Robin and Marian together. The outlaws laughed.

Friar Tuck married them early one beautiful morning under the old oak tree and a big wedding celebration followed. Marian became Robin's wife and they lived happily in Sherwood Forest.

UNDERSTANDING THE TEXT

1 COMPREHENSION CHECK
Match the two parts of the sentences.

1. ☐ Robin Hood, Marian and Mark Fitzwater
2. ☐ Sir Guy of Gisbourne was a rich nobleman
3. ☐ Marian was very upset because
4. ☐ Marian told her brother that
5. ☐ Mark had a clever idea
6. ☐ When Marian got to Sherwood Forest
7. ☐ The beggar told Marian
8. ☐ Marian decided to
9. ☐ When Marian took off her helmet
10. ☐ Robin Hood had to disguise himself
11. ☐ There was a big celebration

A she wanted to run away from home.
B she met a beggar.
C played together when they were children.
D fight the beggar and she won.
E she didn't want to marry Sir Guy of Gisbourne.
F when he went to Nottingham.
G who wanted to marry Marian Fitzwater.
H and helped Marian disguise herself as a knight.
I after the wedding.
J to leave the forest.
K Robin recognised her and she recognised him.

T: GRADE 4

2 SPEAKING – FOOD
There were all kinds of good food at Robin and Marian's wedding celebration. Talk about your favourite food with a partner. Ask and answer these questions.

1. What is your favourite food?
2. Where do you usually eat it?
3. Who does the cooking in your family?
4. How often do you go out to eat with your friends?
5. What is your favourite restaurant?

3 VOCABULARY

A Read the description and write the correct word. There's an example at the beginning.

0 a knight wears this on his head : h e l m e t
1 very bad : e _ _ _
2 change your appearance : d _ _ _ _ _ _ _
3 very poor person : b _ _ _ _ _
4 argument or disagreement : q _ _ _ _ _ _
5 a bad, scary dream : n _ _ _ _ _ _ _ _
6 very surprised : a _ _ _ _ _

B Use the words in part 'A' to complete the sentences below.

1 The ………..in the forest was Robin Hood.
2 The Sheriff's worst ……………was Robin Hood.
3 Friar Tuck had a …………..with the head of the abbey.
4 When Marian took off her …………..Robin recognised her.
5 Mark helped Marian ………….. herself as a knight.
6 Robin was …………..when Marian took off her helmet.
7 The Sheriff of Nottingham was an ……..man.

4 WRITING

You are Marian and you want to write a letter to your father before going to Sherwood Forest. Tell him:

- why you're leaving
- where you're going
- about your disguise
- that you're sorry to leave

Write your letter in about 100 words. Start like this:

> Dear Father,
>
> When you read this letter I'll be far away. You told me that I must marry Sir Guy of Gisbourne, but I don't love him ……

BEFORE YOU READ

1 LISTENING

Listen to part of Chapter Four and choose the correct answer – A, B or C.

1 Many young men hated the Sheriff of Nottingham
   - A ☐ because he was very rich.
   - B ☐ and stole his money.
   - C ☐ and joined the outlaws of Sherwood Forest.

2 The Sheriff of Nottingham's men
   - A ☐ were angry with King John.
   - B ☐ were afraid of Robin Hood and didn't want to go to Sherwood Forest.
   - C ☐ loved Robin Hood dearly.

3 King John was pleased with the Sheriff of Nottingham
   - A ☐ because he decided to go and capture Robin Hood.
   - B ☐ and gave him one hundred pieces of gold.
   - C ☐ because he captured Robin Hood.

4 The Sheriff of Nottingham did not see the outlaws
   - A ☐ and quickly returned to Nottingham Castle.
   - B ☐ because they were hiding in the treetops.
   - C ☐ because it was early in the morning and they were sleeping.

5 When the outlaws saw the Sheriff of Nottingham,
   - A ☐ they wanted to kill him.
   - B ☐ they started running away.
   - C ☐ they hid in the treetops.

6 The Sheriff of Nottingham did not want
   - A ☐ to talk to the outlaws.
   - B ☐ to give Robin his gold, money and jewels.
   - C ☐ to take off his clothes.

CHAPTER **FOUR**

The Cowardly[1] Sheriff

As time passed Robin Hood became famous everywhere. He became the hero of the people and they loved him dearly. Many people called him Robin, Sheriff of Sherwood Forest or Saint Robin.

Many young men who hated the sheriff of Nottingham's cruelty joined the outlaws of Sherwood Forest. They were loyal[2] to their leader, Robin Hood. King John and the sheriff of Nottingham knew this and were very angry.

'What's wrong with your men? Why can't they capture Robin Hood?' asked King John to the sheriff of Nottingham.

'They're afraid of him and his outlaws,' said the sheriff angrily. 'None of them want to go to Sherwood Forest.'

1. **cowardly** : afraid of everything.   2. **loyal** : faithful.

Robin Hood

'What stupid cowards!' cried King John. 'My people hate me and they love Robin Hood! We have to do something. I offered to pay one hundred pieces of gold for that outlaw, dead or alive! But no one has captured him yet.'

'I know what to do,' said the sheriff seriously. 'I'll go to Sherwood Forest alone and capture him myself. I'm not afraid of anyone!'

'Good luck to you!' said King John, who was very pleased.

The Sheriff of Nottingham left for Sherwood Forest early one morning. He rode through Sherwood Forest but didn't see anyone for a long time and he began feeling afraid. Suddenly a group of men jumped down from the treetops – they were the outlaws.

'Goodness, what's happening!' cried the sheriff, whose face was white with fear. The outlaws stood in a big circle around the sheriff and his horse and they pointed their swords at him.

'Good morning, sir!' said Will Scarlett. 'Welcome to Sherwood Forest.'

'What's the sheriff of Nottingham doing in *our* forest?' asked Much.

'Well, what should we do with this kind, honest gentleman?' said Little John laughing.

'Let's kill him!' shouted the outlaws.

'Oh, please, don't hurt me – don't kill me!' said the sheriff, his voice shaking. 'I'll give you everything I have.'

Little John and the other outlaws laughed at the cowardly sheriff and said, 'Let's take him to our leader Robin Hood…'

'Oh, no, please, don't take me to Robin Hood!' said the sheriff, who was ready to cry.

The Cowardly Sheriff

'Don't worry, Robin Hood will invite you to eat with us here in the forest,' said Little John.

'But I'm not hungry,' said the sheriff. 'I want to go home; please let me go. I'll give you a lot of money, gold and jewels.'

'Get off your horse and start walking, you old butcher!' cried Will Scarlett.

'Let's kill him right now!' the outlaws cried. 'That's what he deserves!'

'No, let's take him to Robin Hood first,' said Little John, leading the way through the forest.

When Robin Hood saw the sheriff he wanted to kill him but Maid Marian stopped him.

'Robin, we're not butchers like him and King John,' said Maid Marian. 'We're good, honest people.'

Robin thought for a moment and said, 'Marian's right.' Then he looked at the sheriff and said, 'You're disgusting!'

The sheriff was so frightened he couldn't speak, and the outlaws laughed at him.

'Alright, sit down and eat a meal with us, sheriff,' said Robin. 'And after the meal we have a big surprise for you.'

'I...I'm not hungry, really!' said the sheriff, looking at the outlaws.

'Sit down and eat!' cried Little John.

The sheriff ate very little and at the end of the meal Robin looked at him and said, 'Give us everything you have – gold, money, jewels! Then take off your clothes – all of them!'

'I can give you my gold, my money and my jewels, but please let me keep my clothes,' said the sheriff.

Robin Hood

'No, you can't keep your clothes,' said Robin angrily. 'Take them off immediately.'

'But without my clothes I'm...*naked*!'[3] said the sheriff. 'And I'm cold.'

Will Scarlett laughed and said, 'The butcher's cold! You deserve a worse punishment, sheriff – much worse! You've been cruel and dishonest with the poor people of Nottingham. You're a terrible man!'

'And you're a big coward!' cried Little John.

'Get on your horse and go back to Nottingham naked!' cried Robin Hood, as the outlaws and Marian laughed loudly.

The sheriff left Sherwood Forest naked and he was furious. When he got to Nottingham the people who saw him couldn't stop laughing. Many of them went to call their friends, 'Come and see the sheriff of Nottingham – he's naked!'

Men, women and children all stood in the streets pointing to the naked sheriff – they couldn't believe their eyes.

'I have to capture Robin Hood and kill him! *But how*?' thought the sheriff as he rode through the streets of Nottingham. 'I'll never forget this awful day, *never*.'

---

3. **naked** : with no clothes on.

UNDERSTANDING THE TEXT

1 COMPREHENSION CHECK

Choose the correct answer – A, B, C or D. There is an example at the beginning.

Robin Hood (**0**) ..B... the hero of the people (**1**) .... admired and loved him. He and his outlaws helped and protected them. King John and the Sheriff of Nottingham were (**2**) .... angry because they couldn't (**3**) .... Robin Hood and his outlaws. The Sheriff's men were (**4**) .... of Robin Hood and his outlaws, so the Sheriff decided to go to Sherwood Forest alone. King John was pleased.

At first the Sheriff (**5**) .... through the forest and didn't see (**6**) .... But suddenly the outlaws jumped down (**7**) .... the treetops and pointed their swords at him. They (**8**) .... the cowardly Sheriff to Robin Hood and he was white with (**9**) .... He had to eat with Robin and the outlaws and then he had to give them his money and jewels, and take (**10**) .... all his clothes.

(**11**) .... laughed at the naked Sheriff and when he got (**12**) .... to Nottingham crowds of people in the street couldn't stop laughing at him. He was furious.

0	A be	(B) became	C becoming	D were
1	A that	B they	C whom	D who
2	A very	B many	C much	D lots
3	A take	B bring	C capture	D capturing
4	A scary	B afraid	C frightening	D terror
5	A rode	B ride	C ridden	D riding
6	A something	B someone	C any	D anyone
7	A at	B from	C to	D on
8	A got	B made	C took	D caught
9	A afraid	B scared	C frightened	D fear
10	A out	B off	C on	D of
11	A everyone	B every	C anyone	D none
12	A return	B arrive	C back	D behind

2 NOTICES

Read each notice. What does it say? Choose the best answer – A, B or C.

1

BIG REWARD!
100 pieces of gold. For any information about Robin Hood last seen in Sherwood Forest

- A ☐ Robin Hood will receive one hundred pieces of gold for any information.
- B ☐ Robin Hood will give you one hundred pieces of gold for any information.
- C ☐ You will receive one hundred pieces of gold for any information about Robin Hood.

2

WANTED
Qualified guards for the king's treasure. Must be strong and have at least five years experience. If interested talk to the Sheriff of Nottingham.

- A ☐ The king is looking for guards for his treasure.
- B ☐ Strong guards must work for the king for five years.
- C ☐ Talk to the Sheriff of Nottingham if you are interested in treasures.

3

KNIGHTS
Please tie up your horses outside the south castle walls before entering the east castle gate.

- A ☐ Horses can enter the castle from the east castle gate.
- B ☐ Knights must leave their horses outside the south castle walls.
- C ☐ Knights must enter the castle with their horses through the east castle gate.

4

CAUTION!
Broken bridge over Blue River! People not allowed beyond this point.

- A ☐ All people must proceed with caution beyond this point.
- B ☐ If you want to see Blue River you must go beyond this point.
- C ☐ People must not go any further.

PROJECT ON THE WEB

Let's visit Nottingham!

Connect to the Internet and search for information about Nottingham.

Have the class work in groups and click on the heading on the left-hand column and choose Photos of Nottingham to look at and comment. Which places would your students like to visit and why?

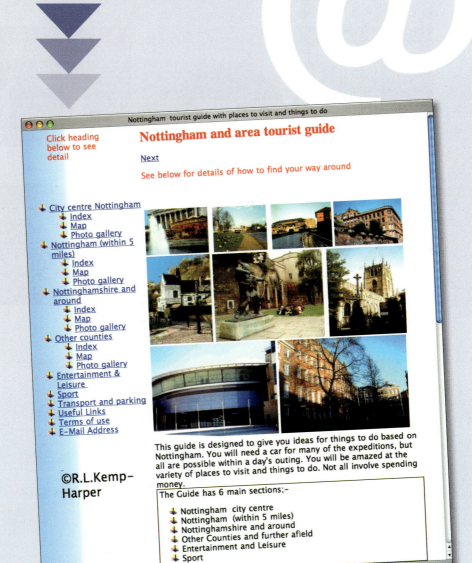

BEFORE YOU READ

1 LISTENING

 Listen to the first part of Chapter Five and choose the correct picture – A, B or C.

1   Where did the Sheriff of Nottingham go the next day?

A

B

C

2   What kind of contest did the Sheriff want to organise?

A

B

C

3   What month was it?

A

B

C

4   What is the prize?

A

B

C

CHAPTER **FIVE**

The Archery[1] Contest

he next day the sheriff of Nottingham rode to the castle to talk to King John. He was worried because he didn't know what to tell the king about this unlucky adventure in Sherwood Forest.

'Well, have you captured Robin Hood and his outlaws?' asked the king, who was anxiously waiting for him.

'No, I haven't captured Robin Hood yet!' said the sheriff.

'What!' cried the king, his face red with anger. 'Do you mean he's still a free man?'

'Yes, and the people of Nottingham are laughing at me,' said the sheriff angrily.

The sheriff explained everything that happened in Sherwood Forest to King John. Both men were furious and didn't know what

1. archery :

Robin Hood

to do. The sheriff started walking around the throne room thinking of a plan.

'I have an idea,' said the sheriff slowly.

'I hope it's a good one!' said the king, angrily.

'I know how we can finally capture Robin Hood,' said the sheriff. 'He loves contests and competitions. Let's have a big archery contest here in Nottingham. It's the month of May and the weather is warm and sunny. The best archers always come to the contest and the prize for the winner will be the famous silver arrow.'

'But Robin Hood won't come because he knows we're looking for him,' said one of the sheriff's men.

'No, he'll come!' said King John excitedly. 'Robin Hood is the best archer in the region and every archer wants to win the silver arrow. I know he'll be there and we'll be ready to capture him.'

'He'll probably come disguised, but my men will recognise him and arrest him,' said the sheriff. 'This time he won't escape!'

'No, this time he mustn't escape!' said King John, looking at the sheriff. 'Robin Hood is your responsibility!'

The sheriff of Nottingham walked out of the castle angrily and called his best messengers. They came quickly and listened to him.

'Tomorrow morning you must get on your horses and ride to every village and every home in the area, and tell the people about the new archery contest,' said the sheriff. 'It will take place next Saturday outside the castle walls and it will be a great day of fun, games, music and archery. Our generous King John will offer food and drink to all. All the best archers are invited to the contest and the prize will be … the silver arrow!'

'Oh, the silver arrow!' exclaimed the messengers.

'How exciting,' said one of the messengers. 'I'll tell my brother James and my cousin Henry who are excellent archers.'

The Archery Contest

'Yes,' said another young messenger, 'and I'll tell my father and uncle – they're the best archers in our village.'

'Make sure you tell everyone!' said the sheriff, smiling to himself.

The messengers rode everywhere and told everyone about the archery contest. People were excited and started making plans. The archers started practising with targets [2] in the forest, and the ladies started getting their best dresses ready. The children were happy because they wanted to play new games and have fun.

Friar Tuck heard about the archery contest and he told Robin Hood and the outlaws.

As soon as Robin heard the news about the contest, he was happy and excited. 'The silver arrow! It's a wonderful prize for an archer. I'm the best archer in the region and I know I can win the silver arrow. I have to go.'

'It's a trap, Robin!' cried Marian. 'Please don't go. The sheriff of Nottingham knows that you'll go and he'll kill you!'

'Marian is right, Robin,' said Friar Tuck. 'It's very dangerous for you because it's a trap.' [3]

'Everyone knows you're the best archer in the area,' said Will Scarlett. 'You don't need to go to the archery contest and win the silver arrow.'

Robin thought for a moment and then said, 'No, I can't refuse a challenge, I have to go. I'll disguise myself as a peasant and no one will recognise me.'

'We'll come to protect you, Robin!' said the outlaws.

'That's a good idea,' said Robin. 'You can come disguised as peasants, too, and stay in the crowd.'

2. **target** :   3. **trap** : (here) a trick to catch someone.

'We'll stay in the crowd but we'll be ready to fight if necessary,' said Will Scarlett.

'Yes, we will,' said Much and the others.

'Please be careful, Robin,' said Marian.

One sunny Saturday morning in the middle of May, Robin Hood and his outlaws went to Nottingham to the archery contest disguised as peasants. There were colourful flags everywhere and the castle square was full of men, women and children. They were talking, laughing, eating and drinking. There

was music and games in the square for the children. It was an exciting day.

The sheriff of Nottingham was standing on the castle wall watching the contest. He was looking for the winner because he knew it was Robin Hood.

All around the big castle square there were difficult targets and the archers tried to hit them, but it wasn't easy. There were a lot of excellent archers at the contest but the best one was a young peasant in a red cloak and hood. He was able to hit the middle of

Robin Hood

all the most difficult targets and he won the silver arrow. The crowd cheered happily.

'Did you see the peasant with the red jacket and hood?' asked a lady to her husband.

'Yes, I've never seen a better archer,' said her husband. 'I wonder who he is?'

'He hit the middle of all the most difficult targets,' said another man. 'He deserves the silver arrow.'

When the sheriff saw the peasant with the red jacket and hood he cried, 'Guards! Stop that peasant with the red jacket! He's the outlaw Robin Hood – our worst enemy! Stop him!'

The guards immediately ran to capture Robin but his outlaws attacked the guards with their swords. There was a big fight and Robin and his men won, and the guards ran away. Robin and his men left the castle square quickly and returned to Sherwood Forest.

Marian was delighted to see Robin return with the silver arrow. That evening there was a big celebration in Sherwood Forest and the hero of the evening was Robin Hood, who was cheered by everyone.

UNDERSTANDING THE TEXT

1 COMPREHENSION CHECK
Answer the following questions.

1. Why did the Sheriff of Nottingham go to talk to King John?
2. Why were the people of Nottingham laughing at the Sheriff of Nottingham?
3. What was the Sheriff's idea to capture Robin Hood?
4. What did the Sheriff tell his messengers to do?
5. Who told Robin Hood about the contest?
6. What did Robin Hood say when he heard the news?
7. What did Marian and Friar Tuck say?
8. Why were the outlaws going to the contest?
9. Describe the castle square on the day of the contest.
10. What happened when the Sheriff saw the peasant with the red jacket?

2 OPPOSITES
What are the opposites of the words in the box? Complete the sentences with the opposites of each of the words below.

| easy | slowly | no one | worst | boring | careless |
| terrible | safe | inside | unhappy | | |

1. The archery contest took place ……………………… the castle walls.
2. It was a very ……………………… day.
3. The archer with the red jacket and hood hit the most ……………………… targets.
4. The Sheriff said, 'Go to all the villages and tell ……………………… about the archery contest.'
5. Robin Hood and his outlaws left the castle square ……………………… and returned to the forest.
6. The silver arrow was a ……………………… prize.
7. The children of the village were ……………………… because they wanted to play games.
8. Marian told Robin to be ……………………… .
9. Only the ……………………… archers went to the contest.
10. The archery contest was a ……………………… place for Robin Hood.

'YES, I'VE NEVER SEEN A BETTER ARCHER,' SAID HER HUSBAND.

We often use *ever/never* with the present perfect.
We use *ever* in questions, it means 'at any time up to now'.
Have you ever studied music?

Never means 'not ever' and we use it with a positive verb.
We've never studied music.

3 PRESENT PERFECT

Complete the sentences with *ever* or *never*.

1 Marian has ……………… been late before.
2 Has she ……………… ridden a horse?
3 Have the outlaws ……………… been to the castle?
4 Friar Tuck has ……………… fought with a sword.
5 January has ……………… been a hot month.
6 Have you ……………… slept in a cave?
7 I have ……………… been to Sherwood Forest.
8 Have you ……………… swum in a river?

4 CHARACTERS

Match the characters below to what they said. Some characters can be used more than once.

1 Marian   3 Will Scarlett   5 Sheriff of Nottingham
2 King John   4 Robin Hood   6 a messenger

A ☐ 'Stop that peasant with the red jacket!'
B ☐ 'We'll stay in the crowd but we'll be ready to fight if necessary.'
C ☐ 'It's a trap, Robin!'
D ☐ 'Make sure you tell everyone!'
E ☐ 'Robin Hood is your responsibility!'
F ☐ 'Do you mean he's still a free man?'
G ☐ 'No, I can't refuse a challenge, I'll go.'
H ☐ 'I'll tell my father and uncle—they're the best archers in our village.'
I ☐ 'I know he'll be there and we'll be ready to capture him.'

5 VOCABULARY

Read the definition and write the word. One of the letters of the word is given.

1. a trick to catch someone: _ _ a _
2. with no clothes on : _ _ _ e _
3. faithful : _ o _ _ _
4. afraid of everything: _ _ _ _ r _ _ _
5. a competition : _ _ n _ _ _ _
6. people who work on farms : p _ _ _ _ _ _ _
7. a person who is not your friend : _ _ e _ _
8. soldiers of the king : _ u _ _ _ _

T: GRADE 4

6 SPEAKING: WEEKEND/SEASONAL ACTIVITIES

The archery contest was a common seasonal activity in England during the Middle Ages. What typical weekend or seasonal activities take place in your area? Talk with a partner and ask and answer the following questions.

1. What activity do you enjoy the most and why?
2. What equipment, if any, do you need for your activity?
3. Do you do this activity with your friends?
4. Are you good at this activity?
5. Do you plan to continue with this activity for a long time? Why? Why not?

Siege of a fortified town, 15th century, unknown artist.

Archery

11 The longbow became the most common weapon in medieval England, and it was used throughout Europe too. This weapon, which was almost as tall as the archer, could send an arrow 180 metres at great speed. It took years of practice and strong arms to become a good archer. The best archers could shoot up to sixteen arrows in a minute and they were very accurate. All Englishmen knew something about archery and the best archers were admired and respected. Archery contests were very popular in medieval times and the winner of the contest became a kind of hero.

In medieval England archers were the most important part of the English army. During a battle noblemen fought as knights on their horses, while ordinary men fought as archers and foot soldiers.[1] Skilled archers could defeat even the best knights. English archers won many battles for their country against the traditional enemy, France, such as the Battle of Agincourt of 1415. The longbow was used for hunting, too, although it wasn't easy.

The Battle of Agincourt (19th century).

1. **foot soldier** : an unimportant man who fights in a battle but does not ride a horse.

Longbows were made by a craftsman called a bowyer. He made them from the wood of the yew tree, which was light and strong. Bowstrings were made of twine which was made from the flax[2] plants.

The arrowheads were made of iron or steel and had different shapes for different uses. Broad arrowheads were used for hunting, while narrower arrowheads were used in battle to go through the knights' armour. Sometimes arrows had feathers tied to them to make them fly straighter.

Today archery is a competitive sport and an important part of the Olympic Games. Although the bows are a bit different, the skill remains the same.

1 COMPREHENSION CHECK
Answer these questions.

1. How far could an arrow travel?
2. How many arrows could a skilled archer shoot in a minute?
3. What was the difference between a knight and an archer during a battle?
4. Who made longbows and what did he use?
5. What were arrowheads made of?
6. What was the purpose of feathers on an arrow?

2. flax :

PROJECT ON THE WEB

Let's learn more about how the Olympic Games started!

Connect to the Internet and search for information about the ancient Olympic Games.

Work in small groups and read about these topics:

1 The Olympic Games
2 The statue of Zeus
3 What was the Sacred Truce?
4 Events at the games
5 Spectators
6 Women at Olympia

BEFORE YOU READ

PET

1 LISTENING

Listen to part of Chapter Six and choose the correct answer – A, B or C.

1. When did Marian and Robin go for walks in the forest?
   - A ☐ in the spring.
   - B ☐ in the summer.
   - C ☐ in the afternoon.

2. What did they hear?
   - A ☐ music
   - B ☐ someone crying
   - C ☐ a loud noise

3. What was Alan a'Dale's song like?
   - A ☐ happy
   - B ☐ funny
   - C ☐ sad

4. Who did Alan a'Dale love?
   - A ☐ Marian
   - B ☐ Alice
   - C ☐ a princess

5. Where was the wedding planned?
   - A ☐ in Nottingham
   - B ☐ at King John's castle
   - C ☐ at Papplewick Church

6. Who interrupted the wedding ceremony?
   - A ☐ Alan a'Dale
   - B ☐ the bishop
   - C ☐ Robin Hood

2 READING PICTURES

Look at the picture on pages 68-69 and answer the following questions.

1. Describe the scene and the people. Where are they? What are they doing?
2. Who is the man sitting near the river? What is he doing?
3. You can see a bird in this picture. There was a bird in the picture on page 39, too – what is the difference between the two birds?

CHAPTER **SIX**
Alice and Alan

Robin and Marian liked going for walks in the forest early in the morning in the summer months. Marian liked picking wild flowers and listening to the birds sing. As they were walking through the forest one warm morning in July they heard music.

'Listen, Robin,' said Marian, 'someone in the forest is playing the lyre.'[1]

'Yes, I can hear it,' said Robin. 'Who can it be?'

Marian and Robin walked towards the river and saw a thin young man sitting on the grass. He was playing the lyre and singing a sad song.

> 'My beautiful love is lost forever
> And never shall I hold her in my arms...
> Never, never, never...'

1. **lyre** :

Marian and Robin listened to the sad song and then Robin asked, 'Who are you, young man? Why are you singing this sad song?'

'Good day, sir. My name is Alan of Barnsdale but everyone calls me Alan a'Dale,' said the young man sadly. 'I'm singing this sad song because I love a beautiful girl named Alice. I've always loved her and she's always loved me. But I'm a poor man and her father wants her to marry a rich old baron.' [2]

2. **baron** : the title of a nobleman.

'Oh,' said Marian, 'I'm very sorry.' She remembered her similar situation.

'Alice is going to get married tomorrow at noon at Papplewick Church and I'll never see her again,' said Alan a'Dale. 'I'm very unhappy and there's nothing I can do.'

'Perhaps there's something we can do to help you and Alice,' said Robin, looking at Marian.

Alan a'Dale jumped up from the grass, dropped his lyre and looked at Robin. 'Can you really help us?' he asked excitedly.

Robin Hood

'Yes,' said Robin. 'I'm sure I can.'

'But who are you, sir?' asked Alan a'Dale.

'I'm Robin Hood and this is my wife, Marian.'

'Robin Hood!' exclaimed Alan a'Dale. 'I've already heard about you; you're the hero of Sherwood Forest! Everyone talks about your brave adventures.'

'Come with me, Alan a'Dale,' said Robin. 'My men and I can help you. I'm thinking of a clever plan.'

'Oh, thank you, sir!' said Alan a'Dale. 'Thank you!'

Early the next morning Robin Hood sent his best archers to Papplewick Church. He told them to hide inside the small church and all around it. Robin, Alan a'Dale and Friar Tuck disguised themselves as poor peasants. Then they walked to Papplewick Church and sat down.

At noon the bishop [3] and the rich old baron walked into the church. The rich old baron was wearing fine new clothes and expensive jewels. A bit later Alice got to the church with her father. She was a beautiful young girl with a lovely white dress and flowers in her long hair. But her face was pale and her eyes were very sad. She never smiled.

When the bishop began the marriage ceremony Robin suddenly stood up and said loudly, 'My lord, an old man cannot marry this young woman. Winter cannot marry Spring.'

The bishop was surprised and turned around to look at the people in the church. 'Who has just spoken?'

'I have just spoken, sir,' said Robin Hood. 'There is no love between this old man and this young girl – you cannot marry them! Marriage is for people who are in love.'

---

3. **bishop** : an important religious man.

Alice and Alan

'What! Sit down and be silent!' cried the bishop angrily. 'Guards, arrest that stupid peasant! Take him out of the church!'

Robin's men immediately stood up and pointed their bows and arrows at the guards who were frightened.

'If you move we'll kill you,' said Will Scarlett.

'Now leave the church quickly, all of you!' cried Little John, looking at the bishop and the guards.

The bishop ran out of the church followed by the rich old baron and the guards.

Then Robin went to Alice and asked her, 'Is there anyone here you want to marry?'

She saw Alan a'Dale and ran to him. 'Alan, my love! You're the only man I want to marry!'

'My dear Alice, you're the only girl I want to marry!'

Alice and Alan a'Dale were delighted to see each other and Friar Tuck married them the same day at Papplewick Church. Everyone then returned to Sherwood Forest and enjoyed the wedding festivities. Alan a'Dale and Alice decided to live in Sherwood Forest with Robin, Marian and the outlaws.

UNDERSTANDING THE TEXT

1 COMPREHENSION CHECK

Read the sentences below and decide if each sentence is correct or incorrect. If it is correct, mark A. If is not correct, mark B.

		A	B
1	Wild flowers grew in Sherwood Forest during the summer.	☐	☐
2	Robin and Marian went walking in the forest because they heard music.	☐	☐
3	Alan a'Dale was tall and strong and played the lyre.	☐	☐
4	Alan a'Dale was very sad because Alice was going to marry someone else.	☐	☐
5	Alan a'Dale was in the forest because he was looking for Robin Hood.	☐	☐
6	On the wedding day Robin's best archers were hiding inside Papplewick Church.	☐	☐
7	Robin Hood told the bishop that marriage was only for people who are in love.	☐	☐
8	The bishop was a friend of Friar Tuck.	☐	☐
9	The guards arrested Robin's outlaws and they had to leave the church.	☐	☐
10	Alice and Alan a'Dale became husband and wife.	☐	☐

2 SENTENCE TRANSFORMATION

For each question complete the second sentence so that it means the same as the first, using no more than three words. There's an example at the beginning (0).

0   Alan a'Dale heard nothing, except the sound of the lyre.

Alan a'Dale .... *didn't hear* .... anything except the sound of the lyre.

1   Little John is going away tomorrow and he wants to see Robin Hood first.

Little John wants to see Robin Hood .... away tomorrow.

2   Everyone was silent.

Nobody .... anything.

3   It's too cold to swim in the stream.
    It isn't .... to swim in the stream.
4   The town of Nottingham was near us.
    The town of Nottingham was .... from us.
5   It was too dark to see anything in the forest.
    It wasn't light .... anything.
6   There was very little food left.
    There .... left.

AS THEY WERE WALKING THROUGH THE FOREST ONE WARM MORNING IN JULY THEY HEARD MUSIC.

The verb *'were walking'* is in the Past Continuous tense. We use this tense for:
- an action in the past that has a duration
- an action that was interrupted by another action expressed by the Past Simple

3 PAST SIMPLE AND PAST CONTINUOUS

Put the verbs in brackets in the Past Continuous (*was/were* + verb *-ing*) or Past Simple form.

1   Robin and Marian (walk) .... in the forest when they (meet) .... Alan a'Dale.
2   Alan a'Dale (think) .... about Alice when Robin and Marian (see) .... him.
3   While Robin (talk) .... to Alan a'Dale, Marian (pick) .... some wild flowers.
4   It (be) .... a wonderful day because everyone (celebrate) .... the wedding in the forest.
5   While the Sheriff of Nottingham (ride) .... in the forest, the outlaws (attack) .... him.
6   Will Scarlett and Much (hunt) .... in the forest when they (hear) .... a loud noise.
7   The outlaws (hunt) ....in the forest when it (start)............raining.
8   While Friar Tuck (fish)............in the river, the Sheriff's men (see)...........him.

4 WORD FORMATION

Complete the table. Use your dictionary only if necessary.

NOUN	VERB
0 entrance	enter
1 choice	
2 arrival	
3 disappearance	
4 explanation	
5 information	
6 marriage	
7 agreement	
8 improvement	
9 announcement	
10 invitation	

5 SYNONYMS

Synonyms are words which have similar meanings. For example, unhappy is a synonym of sad. Choose three synonyms from the words in the box for each of the words in the table. Use your dictionary only if necessary.

attractive affluent depressed ecstatic slim excellent
great fantastic glad handsome joyful miserable pretty
skinny prosperous slender unhappy wealthy

rich	
beautiful	
thin	
happy	
sad	
wonderful	

6 DO YOU REMEMBER THESE WORDS?
Complete the crossword below.

Across
2.
4. very bad
7. an important religious person
8.
9. a very small river
12.
13.
14. not honest

Down
1. very unkind
3. people who buy and sell things
5. Alan's wife
6.
8. a nobleman
10. Marian's brother
11.
12.

King Richard's Crusade

King Richard the Lionheart

King Richard the Lionheart became King of England in 1189 and after only seven months he decided to go on a crusade. A crusade was a religious war to recapture the city of Jerusalem in the Holy Land. At that time many European kings went on crusades because it was considered the bravest thing a king could do. The French king Philip Augustus and the German king Frederick Barbarossa joined Richard on this third crusade.

King Richard organized a fleet [1] of over one hundred ships to take his army to the Holy Land and he left for the crusade in 1190. While he was away his greedy brother John ruled England, causing a lot of serious problems with his people and his noblemen. No one liked Prince John because he wasn't interested in ruling his country and never followed the laws.

King Richard's crusade was a difficult one. Frederick Barbarossa

1. **fleet** : a big number of ships.

Map of the routes of the crusaders.

died at sea before arriving in the Holy Land and Philip Augustus became very ill when he arrived and had to return to France. Therefore, King Richard and his army had to fight alone, winning many important battles. He conquered the island of Cyprus and the coastal cities of Acre, Jaffa and Ascalon, but he could not recapture Jerusalem.

King Richard made an agreement with the great Muslim leader Saladin, who was a wise and noble man, that the Muslims could have control of Jerusalem but that pilgrims [2] could visit it freely.

In 1192, during his return journey, Richard was captured by Duke Leopold of Austria and was put in prison in Durnstein Castle, just

2. **pilgrims** : people who travel to a place for religious reasons.

outside Vienna, where he spent more than a year. Richard had to pay a huge amount of money to be free. He finally returned to England in 1194 after four years. He ruled England for a short time because he had to go to fight in France where he was killed in battle in 1199.

Today in London there is a beautiful statue of King Richard the Lionheart outside the Houses of Parliament.

1 COMPREHENSION CHECK

Choose the correct answer – A, B or C.

1 When did King Richard leave to go on a crusade?
   A ☐ in 1192
   B ☐ in 1190
   C ☐ in 1189

2 Who joined King Richard on the crusade?
   A ☐ King John
   B ☐ King Frederick Barbarossa and King Philip Augustus
   C ☐ Duke Leopold

3 Who ruled England while King Richard was away?
   A ☐ King Richard's brother
   B ☐ Duke Leopold
   C ☐ no one

4 King Richard made an important agreement with
   A ☐ the great Muslim leader Saladin.
   B ☐ the people of Jerusalem.
   C ☐ with Duke Leopold.

5 Where was Durnstein Castle?
   A ☐ in Germany
   B ☐ in Austria
   C ☐ on the island of Cyprus

BEFORE YOU READ

1 LISTENING

Listen to part of Chapter Seven and choose the correct answer – A, B or C.

1 Robin Hood and his men went hunting in the forest and met
   - A ☐ a wild boar.
   - B ☐ a knight.
   - C ☐ a horse.

2 What did the knight ask?
   - A ☐ the name of the territory
   - B ☐ the name of the king
   - C ☐ the name of the forest

3 The knight
   - A ☐ has been out of the country for a long time.
   - B ☐ has been in the forest for a long time.
   - C ☐ hasn't been away much.

4 Robin told him that
   - A ☐ the king's brother and the sheriff of Nottingham were very good people.
   - B ☐ the king's brother and the sheriff of Nottingham were evil people.
   - C ☐ the king's brother and the sheriff of Nottingham were all the taxes.

5 Some poor people died because
   - A ☐ they didn't have anywhere to live.
   - B ☐ they didn't have anything to eat.
   - C ☐ they didn't have enough to eat.

6 King John and his men
   - A ☐ killed Robin's father and took away his house and lands.
   - B ☐ killed Robin's grandfather and took away his house and lands.
   - C ☐ killed Robin's father and gave his house and lands to the poor.

CHAPTER **SEVEN**
A Knight in the Forest

Robin Hood and his men often went hunting for deer, boars and hares in the forest. Late one afternoon while they were hunting Robin saw a knight on a horse riding slowly towards him. Both the horse and the knight were very tired. The knight was wearing the red cross of a crusader.

'Good afternoon, young man!' said the knight. 'What's the name of this forest?'

'This is Sherwood Forest,' said Robin, looking at the knight.

'Welcome to Sherwood Forest, sir!' said Will Scarlett and Much.

'Is this forest yours?' asked the knight, looking around. 'Most of the forests in England belong to the king, don't they?'

Robin and his men started laughing.

'Perhaps I'm wrong,' said the knight, 'and this forest is yours. I've been away on a crusade to the Holy Land for many years and I don't know what's happening in England.'

Robin and the outlaws looked at each other.

A Knight in the Forest

'Let me tell you what's happening, sir,' said Robin. 'Everyone loved good King Richard but he went on a crusade and his greedy brother John now rules England. The wicked sheriff of Nottingham is his best friend and they're both cruel and dishonest. The poor, honest people pay high taxes to the king and his sheriff. They lead a very difficult life and are unhappy. Some people die because they don't have anything to eat.'

'This is terrible!' exclaimed the knight, who was listening carefully.

Robin continued, 'King John and his men killed my father, the Earl of Huntingdon, and I lost my home and my lands in Locksley. I became an outlaw named Robin Hood and many honest men have joined me here in Sherwood Forest. We take from the rich and give to the poor, and we protect women and children.'

'What a situation!' said the knight, who was worried. 'You and your outlaws are doing the right thing.'

'You must be tired and hungry, sir,' said Robin Hood. 'Why don't you have dinner with us this evening?'

'Thank you,' said the knight. 'That's very kind of you!'

That evening the knight sat next to Marian and Robin and enjoyed a delicious meal of roast boar. At the end of the meal Robin stood up and said, 'Let's drink to our good King Richard!'

'And let's drink to his return home!' said Little John.

'Yes, to our good King Richard and to his return home!' cried everyone happily.

Suddenly the knight stood up and said, 'I've been away from England for many years and my hair and beard have become grey. You probably don't recognise me but I'm not a knight...I'm your king, Richard, known as Lionheart, and I've just returned from the Holy Land!'

Robin Hood

There was a moment of silence and Marian, Robin and the outlaws looked at each other. The surprise was too great – they couldn't believe their eyes. King Richard was there with them.

Everyone suddenly stood up and cheered, 'Long live King Richard! Long live England's best king!'

King Richard smiled and said, 'I'm a lucky king because I have loyal people. My brother John and the sheriff of Nottingham have been greedy, cruel and dishonest. I'm very angry and I'm here to punish them and their evil friends. Robin Hood, your home and your lands are yours again. You are now Lord Huntingdon. And all the outlaws are now free men and friends of mine. You can all leave Sherwood Forest tomorrow morning and live as free men.

'Hurrah! Hurrah!' everyone cried.

There was great excitement in Sherwood Forest that night and no one was able to sleep. The next morning Robin Hood, Marian, King Richard and his new friends rode to Nottingham. When the sheriff of Nottingham saw them approaching he got on his horse and galloped away as fast as possible and he never returned.

King John stood on the castle walls and saw his brother Richard approaching with a crowd of happy people. His face became white with fear and he ran back to his secret rooms in the castle.

After King Richard's return, Robin Hood, Marian and Little John went to live in Robin's home in Locksley, where they had a long and happy life. Will Scarlett and Much returned to their villages and their homes. Friar Tuck returned to Fountains Abbey where he led a simple life and helped others.

Some outlaws, who were now free men, became soldiers in King Richard's army, and others looked for new adventures. But everyone had a wonderful memory of the years spent together in Sherwood Forest.

UNDERSTANDING THE TEXT

1 COMPREHENSION CHECK
Choose the correct answer – A, B, C or D.

1 The knight in the forest
   A ☐ was a crusader.
   B ☐ was walking alone.
   C ☐ was hunting for deer and boar.
   D ☐ was galloping on his horse.

2 The poor people and the peasants were unhappy
   A ☐ and left England.
   B ☐ because they had to pay high taxes to the king and the sheriff.
   C ☐ because they couldn't go to the Holy Land.
   D ☐ because they couldn't hunt in the forest.

3 The knight decided to
   A ☐ return to the Holy Land.
   B ☐ go to Nottingham and talk to King John.
   C ☐ stay and have dinner with Robin Hood and the outlaws.
   D ☐ go to Locksley and look for the Earl of Huntingdon.

4 At the end of the delicious meal
   A ☐ the knight returned to Nottingham.
   B ☐ the knight gave Robin some money.
   C ☐ everyone sang songs.
   D ☐ everyone stood up and drank to good King Richard.

5 The knight said he was King Richard
   A ☐ and he wanted to go back to the Holy Land.
   B ☐ and he wanted to punish King John and the Sheriff of Nottingham.
   C ☐ but he didn't want to hurt his brother John.
   D ☐ and a good friend of Robin Hood's father.

6 The next day Robin Hood, Marian and the outlaws left Sherwood Forest
   A ☐ and went to the Holy Land with King Richard.
   B ☐ because they were free men.
   C ☐ and went to live in Nottingham.
   D ☐ and attacked King John's castle.

2 LISTENING

Listen to the recording about King Richard and fill in the information requested.

KING RICHARD

Nickname ....
Date of birth ....
Place of birth ....
Father's name ....
Father's nationality ....
Mother's name ....
Mother's nationality ....
Brothers .... Sisters ....
Hair .... Eyes ....
Languages spoken .... Hobbies ....
Died .... Buried in ....

3 SENTENCE TRANSFORMATION

For each question complete the second sentence so that it means the same as the first. Use no more than three words.

1 King Richard thought the outlaws should leave Sherwood Forest.
   King Richard wanted .... leave Sherwood Forest.

2 The forest has many beautiful trees.
   In the forest .... beautiful trees.

3 Nottingham isn't as big as London.
   Nottingham is .... London.

4 Are these the sheriff's clothes?
   Do these clothes .... sheriff?

5 The old king built part of Nottingham Castle.
   Part of Nottingham Castle .... the old king.

4 SPEAKING: THE HOT SEAT

A chair in front of the class is the 'hot seat'. While you are sitting in this chair you are Robin Hood, Marian, King John or the Sheriff of Nottingham: you must answer as if you were one of these characters. Take turns sitting here. The rest of the class can ask the person in the hot seat any questions. Here are some examples. Then think of some other questions.

Questions for Robin Hood
What did you do when the king killed your father?
Why did you decide to become an outlaw?
How many people's lives have you saved so far?
Where did you learn how to use the bow and arrow?

Questions for Marian
How did you feel when your father wanted you to marry that old man?
How did you manage to disguise yourself as a knight?
Where did you learn to use the sword so well?
Are you happy to be Robin's wife now?

Questions for King John
Why do people call you king when you're a prince?
Why do you make poor people pay high taxes?
Why did you take away their lands?
How will you justify your evil actions to you brother?

Questions for the Sheriff of Nottingham
Why do you hate Robin Hood so much?
Why did you kill his father?
How did you feel when you had to go back to town without clothes?
Where did you run to when King Richard came back?

Questions for Little John
How did you meet Robin Hood?
Did you like him at first? Why or why not?
Who taught you how to fight with the staff?
Why did you leave Barnsdale?

King John

The Magna Carta

When King Richard died in 1199, his brother King John became King of England. He was a cruel, violent man who had absolute power over everyone. He thought only about himself and his possessions, and spent huge amounts of money on his clothes and jewels. He lost most of the lands England had in France and continued taxing his people and barons more and more.

There was practically no justice during King John's rule. He never followed the laws, sent innocent people to prison and often killed them without a reason. King John was extremely unpopular throughout England with his barons, the clergy and the people.

The English barons met secretly and decided to change things. They wrote a document called the Magna Carta and forced King John to sign it in June 1215 at Runnymede, a town in Surrey.

The Magna Carta marked the beginning of democracy in England. It did not grant democracy to the people because the barons wanted to protect their privileges. But it limited the absolute power of the King. It was also the first document that promised certain rights to the people of the kingdom.

The Magna Carta promised two kinds of rights. Some were the rights the king promised to the barons, and the others were the rights the barons promised to the people under them.

For example, one clause [1] said that the king must ask the barons' advice in all important matters. Another clause said that no special taxes could be raised without the barons' agreement. Another very important clause said that *everyone* must respect the law of the land.

The Magna Carta

When King John died in 1216, England was divided by a civil war. He was succeeded by his nine-year-old son who became King Henry III.

1 COMPREHENSION CHECK
Answer these questions.

1. What was King John like?
2. Why was he so unpopular?
3. What did the English barons decide to do?
4. What rights did the Magna Carta promise?
5. Describe the important clauses of the document.

1. **clause** : a part of a document.

PROJECT ON THE WEB

Let's find out more about the Magna Carta and King John!

Connect to the Internet and search for information about the Magna Carta and King John.

You can visit the original Magna Carta at the British Library in London.

Work with a partner and get more information about the Magna Carta and King John, then tell the class what you learned.

Filmography

Scene from *Robin Hood*, 1922.

The legend of Robin Hood has attracted cinema and television audiences for a long time. Look at this list of some of the most important films:

1908: *Robin Hood and his Merry Men* – the first appearance of Robin Hood on the screen (silent film)

1912: *Robin Hood*, starring Robert Frazer (silent film)

1922: *Robin Hood*, starring Douglas Fairbanks

1938: *The adventures of Robin Hood*, starring Errol Flynn

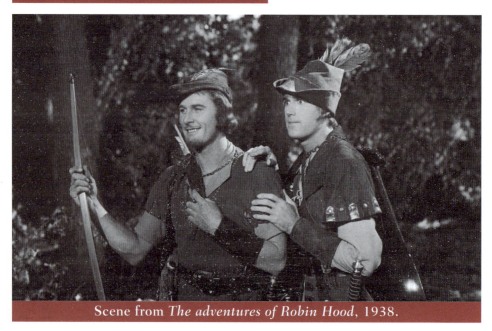

Scene from *The adventures of Robin Hood*, 1938.

1973: *Robin Hood*, directed by Walt Disney – (cartoon)

1976: *Robin and Marian*, starring Sean Connery and Audrey Hepburn

1991: *Robin Hood, Prince of Thieves*, starring Kevin Costner

2010: *Robin Hood*, directed by Ridley Scott, starring Russell Crowe

Numerous TV films about Robin Hood, Marian and the sheriff of Nottingham have also been produced in many countries all over the world.

Scene from *Robin Hood, Prince of Thieves*, 1991.

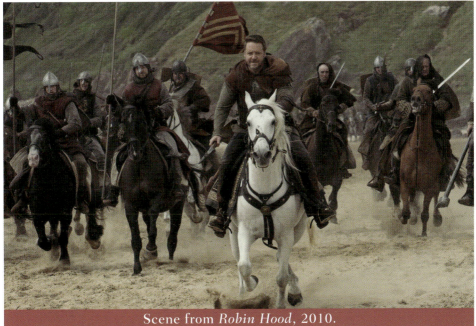

Scene from *Robin Hood*, 2010.

AFTER READING

1 SUMMARY

Read the sentences below and decide if each sentence is correct or incorrect. If it is correct, mark A. If it is not correct, mark B.

  A B

1 King John ruled England during his brother's absence.
2 Robin Hood became an outlaw because he didn't like living in Nottingham.
3 Robin Hood and his outlaws promised to help women, children and the poor.
4 Friar Tuck was a greedy churchman from Fountains Abbey.
5 Little John had to change his name before becoming an outlaw.
6 Travellers had to cross Sherwood Forest on Watling Street.
7 King John promised one hundred pieces of gold to anyone who captured Robin Hood.
8 Mark Fitzwater was Marian's father.
9 Robin Hood and Marian met in the forest but didn't recognise each other at first.
10 Marian lost the fight with the sword against Robin Hood.
11 The Sheriff of Nottingham left Sherwood Forest without his money, gold, jewels and clothes.
12 Robin Hood went to the archery contest disguised as a beggar.
13 Friar Tuck married Alice and Alan a'Dale in Papplewick Church.
14 The knight in the forest was King Richard's brother.
15 Robin Hood and Little John joined King Richard's army and went to the Holy Land.

2 WHO WAS IT?

Read the description of the character and match it with the name. You can use a name more than once.

1. He came from Locksley.
2. He wanted to marry Marian Fitzwater.
3. He won the silver arrow.
4. He was King Richard's brother.
5. He went back to Nottingham naked.
6. She didn't want to marry Sir Guy of Gisbourne.
7. He fought with a wooden staff.
8. He came from Fountains Abbey.
9. He offered one hundred pieces of gold for Robin Hood, dead or alive.
10. He helped Marian disguise herself as a knight.
11. He played the lyre.
12. He went on a crusade to the Holy Land.
13. He married Alice and Alan.

A ☐ ☐ King John.
B ☐ ☐ Alan a'Dale.
C ☐ ☐ Sheriff of Nottingham.
D ☐ ☐ Mark Fitzwater.
E ☐ ☐ Little John.
F ☐ ☐ Sir Guy of Gisbourne.
G ☐ ☐ King Richard.
H ☐ ☐ Marian Fitzwater.
I ☐ ☐ Friar Tuck.
J ☐ ☐ Robin Hood.

1. Who was your favourite character and why?
   ....
   ....
   ....
2. What was your favourite part of the story?
   ....
   ....
   ....

3 PICTURE SUMMARY

Look at the pictures from Robin Hood below. They are not in the right order. Put them in the order in which they appear in the story, and then write a sentence under each picture to summarise what's happening.

A ▢

B ▢

C ▢

D ▢

E ▢

F ▢

4 A GRAPHIC NOVEL

Photocopy these two pages, cut out the pictures and stick them on paper in the right order. Think of words to put in speech or thought bubbles to show what the characters are saying or thinking. Do not use the words that were used in this book! Then write at least one sentence under each picture to narrate what is happening.

This reader uses the **EXPANSIVE READING** approach, where the text becomes a springboard to improve language skills and to explore historical background, cultural connections and other topics suggested by the text.

The new structures introduced in this step of our GREEN APPLE series are listed below. Naturally, structures from lower steps are included too. For a complete list of structures used over all the three steps, see *The Black Cat Guide to Graded Readers*, which is also downloadable at no cost from our website, blackcat-cideb.com.

The vocabulary used at each step is carefully checked against vocabulary lists used for internationally recognised examinations.

Step 2

All the structures used in the previous steps, plus the following:

Verb tenses
Present Perfect Simple: indefinite past with *ever, never* (for experience); indefinite past with *yet, already, still*; recent past with *just*; past action leading to present situation; unfinished past with *for* or *since* (duration form)

Verb forms and patterns
So / neither / nor + auxiliaries in short answers
Question tags (in verb tenses used so far)
Gerunds (verb + -*ing*) as subjects
Verb + object + full infinitive (e.g. *I want you to help*)

Modal verbs
Should (present and future reference): advice
Might (present and future reference): possibility; permission
Don't have to / haven't got to: lack of obligation
Don't need to / needn't: lack of necessity

Types of clause
Defining relative clauses with: *which, that,* zero pronoun
Time clauses introduced by *when, while, until, before, after, as soon as*
Clauses of purpose: *(in order) to* (infinitive of purpose)

Other
Comparative and superlative of adverbs (regular and irregular)